my itty-bitty bio

J.J. Watt

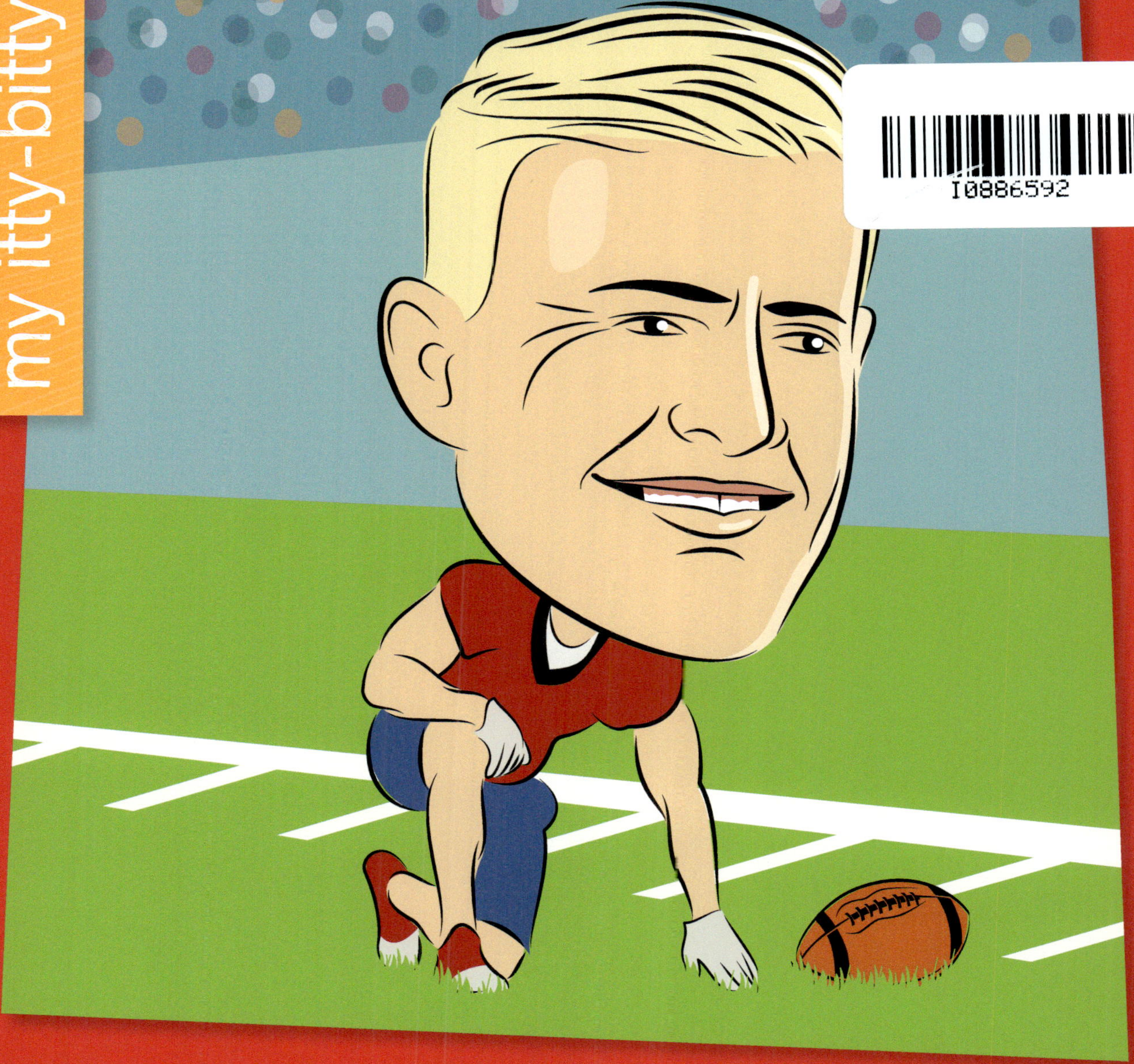

Cherry Lake Press

Published in the United States of America by Cherry Lake Publishing
Ann Arbor, Michigan
www.cherrylakepublishing.com

Reading Adviser: Marla Conn, MS, Ed., Literacy specialist, Read-Ability, Inc.
Book Designer: Jennifer Wahi
Illustrator: Jeff Bane

Photo Credits: ©Alexander Lukatskiy/Shutterstock, 5; ©4 PM production/Shutterstock, 7; ©DardaInna/Shutterstock, 9; ©Jeff Bukowski/Shutterstock, 11, 22; ©Alexander Martinez/Wikimedia/Public Domain, 13; ©Sgt. Staci Miller/Luke Air Force Base/Public Domain, 15; ©Atonaltzin/Shutterstock, 17; ©AMFPhotography/Shutterstock, 19, 23; ©Jeffrey Beall/ Wikimedia/Creative Commons Attribution-Share Alike 3.0 Unported, 21; Jeff Bane, cover, 1, 6, 10, 18

Library of Congress Cataloging-in-Publication Data

Names: Sarantou, Katlin, author. | Bane, Jeff, 1957- illustrator.
Title: J.J. Watt / Katlin Sarantou, Jeff Bane.
Description: Ann Arbor, Michigan : Cherry Lake Publishing, [2020] | Series: My itty-bitty bio | Includes index. | Audience: Grades K-1 | Summary: "The My Itty-Bitty Bio series are biographies for the earliest readers. This book examines the life of J.J. Watt in a simple, age-appropriate way that will help children develop word recognition and reading skills. Includes a table of contents, author biography, timeline, glossary, index, and other informative backmatter"-- Provided by publisher.
Identifiers: LCCN 2019034652 (print) | LCCN 2019034653 (ebook) | ISBN 9781534158788 (hardcover) | ISBN 9781534161085 (paperback) | ISBN 9781534159938 (pdf) | ISBN 9781534162235 (ebook)
Subjects: LCSH: Watt, J. J., 1989---Juvenile literature. | Football players--United States--Biography--Juvenile literature.
Classification: LCC GV939.W362 S27 2020 (print) | LCC GV939.W362 (ebook) | DDC 796.332092 [B]--dc23
LC record available at https://lccn.loc.gov/2019034652
LC ebook record available at https://lccn.loc.gov/2019034653

Printed in the United States of America
Corporate Graphics

table of contents

About the author: Katlin Sarantou grew up in the cornfields of Ohio. She enjoys reading and dreaming of faraway places.

About the illustrator: Jeff Bane and his two business partners own a studio along the American River in Folsom, California, home of the 1849 Gold Rush. When Jeff's not sketching or illustrating for clients, he's either swimming or kayaking in the river to relax.

my story

My name is Justin James Watt.
I'm called J.J.

I was born in Wisconsin on
March 22, 1989.

Minnesota
Fargo
Duluth
Superior
Ironwood
Marquette
Sault
Ste. Marie
Escanaba
Wisconsin
Minneapolis
St-Paul
Menominee
Green
Bay
Eau Claire
Appleton
Luverne
Rochester
Sheboygan
La Crosse
Mason City
Lake Michigan
Ludington
Madison
Milwaukee
Dubuque
Janesville
Iowa
Cedar
Rapids
Rockford
Chicago

Family is really important to me. My middle name is for my grandpa. He taught me to never give up.

I played hockey and football growing up.

I had to choose one. I chose football. But I still like hockey.

What sport do you like best?

I was **drafted** by the Texans in 2011. They're a team in the **NFL**.

My two brothers also play in the NFL. We're on different teams.

I play **defensive end**. I've set records. I've won awards.

WATT
99

I love giving back to my community. I started a **foundation**.

It raises money for after-school programs.

What do you do after school?

These programs help kids have a safe place. They can play sports. They can have fun.

Houston, Texas, was hit by **Hurricane** Harvey. This happened in 2017.

I helped raise money. The money helped rebuild homes.

My **motto** is "Dream big, work hard."

Anything is possible. All you have to do is put in the work.

What would you like to ask me?

timeline

2011

1980

Born 1989

2017

2080

glossary

defensive end (dih-FEN-siv END) a position on a football team; this person defends against passes and tackles players

drafted (DRAFT-id) to be chosen by a sports team

foundation (foun-DAY-shuhn) an organization that gives money to help others

hurricane (HUR-ih-kane) a powerful storm with damaging winds

motto (MAH-toh) a short sentence that states someone's beliefs

NFL (EN EF EL) stands for the National Football League, the organization that teams belong to

index